Contents

Program Explosion

Computer programs are sets of instructions to make a computer work. Since the first programs were written in the 1930s and 1940s, many types of program have been created. Applications are special programs that do specific jobs on a computer.

Keep in touch

Lots of **applications**, from email to video conferencing **programs**, let you communicate with other people.

Speed things up

Many programs help you do jobs faster. Computers are brilliant at maths and can work out problems in a fraction of a second, making them great for tasks in science, finance and engineering.

Application or Program?

All applications are programs or collections of programs that let you do something on your computer. These include word processors, web browsers and and image editing programs. However, other programs also run in the background on your computer. These are not thought of as applications, but have important jobs to do, such as automatically saving files or checking for problems.

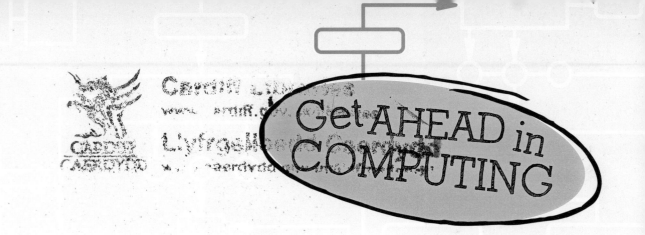

Amazing APPLICATIONS and Perfect PROGRAMS

Clive Gifford

First published in 2016 by Wayland
Copyright © Wayland 2016

Wayland is an imprint of Hachette Children's Group
Part of Hodder & Stoughton
Carmelite House, 50 Victoria Embankment
London EC4Y 0DZ

Commissioning Editor: Debbie Foy
Project Editor: Caroline West (Blue Dragonfly Ltd.)
Designer: Mark Latter (Blue Dragonfly Ltd.)

A catalogue record for this title is available
from the British Library

ISBN: 978 0 7502 9221 4
Library eBook ISBN: 978 0 7502 9220 7
Dewey number: 005.3–dc23
10 9 8 7 6 5 4 3 2 1

Printed in China

An Hachette UK company
www.hachette.co.uk
www.hachettechildrens.co.uk

All images courtesy of Shutterstock.

Note to reader: Words highlighted in bold appear in the
Glossary on page 30. Answers to activities are on page 31.

General and Special Programs

Some programs work on a wide range of machines. For example, a web browser application to view websites might work on different tablets, laptops and desktop PCs. Other programs are written to work on just one device – for example, a program that controls a sports car's engine or makes a particular robot move.

Big brains

Some applications let computers store huge amounts of information. An entire library's worth of data can be stored on a single computer. This means that you can search for certain words or images in seconds.

Get creative!

Computer applications let you do lots of exciting things, such as changing how photographs look or creating cartoons. You can also use applications just for fun. These include media player programs, which let you play music or audio books on a computer device, and computer games. In some games, you can even play against someone on the other side of the world!

TRUE STORY

Mission In Space Some programs are written to work only on one single machine. The Mars Curiosity Rover space robot explores the surface of Mars. Specially written programs help run the controller — the brains of the robot. The Rover's programs contain more than 2.5 million lines of **code**.

Operating Systems

An operating system (OS) is one of the main programs that controls a computer. It lets other programs work with the computer. For example, Windows 8 and MacOS are both types of operating system.

Booting up

When you switch on a computer, tablet or smartphone, there's often a delay before you can use the machine. The computer isn't working slowly, though. Instead, it's whizzing through lots of different tasks, such as checking that its parts are working properly, as well as starting up the **operating system.** This is called the **booting up** process.

In control

Once up and running, the operating system controls the computer. It links all the computer's parts – from its **microprocessor** and memory to its screen and any peripherals. Peripherals are items such as a computer mouse, printer or keyboard that are also connected to the computer.

The operating system deals with opening, closing and deleting files. It decides when programs should run and for how long. It also displays error messages if there are problems.

TRUE STORY

Linux Rules! Although Windows and other operating systems are more well-known, the majority of the world's most powerful computers use an operating system called Linux. At the end of 2013, over 480 of the top 500 supercomputers were using Linux.

How Operating Systems Work

The operating system allows users to run applications such as word processors. Applications communicate with the hardware - the physical parts of the computer - through the operating system.

User

Application
e.g. word processors, web browsers, spreadsheets and games

Operating System
e.g. Windows 8, MacOS

Hardware
e.g. hard disk, mouse, keyboard, etc.

COMPUTER Hero!

Linus Torvalds loved computers as a teenager. In 1991, the young computer student from Finland bought his first PC, but was disappointed with the operating system that came with it… so, he built his own!

Torvalds called his operating system Linux and let other programmers use it for free. Other people began adding to Linux, turning it into a very powerful system. Today, many different versions of Linux are used on lots of devices, including smart TVs and huge supercomputers.

An asteroid discovered in 1996 was named '9793 Torvalds' in Linus' honour!

Handy helpers

Most operating systems do more than just run the computer and all its parts. They also come with other handy programs, which make using a computer easier and allow you to do different jobs. Some of these programs are applications (known as accessories) such as a word processor, calculator and sound recorder.

Utilities

Other programs that may come with an operating system are designed to repair or look after your computer's health. These utility programs let you shrink the size of a file (see page 13) or check the hard disk for any parts that are not storing data properly.

Popular Operating Systems

There are lots of different operating systems. Many computers and smart devices come with an operating system already loaded on the machine, but some people like to install a different one themselves.

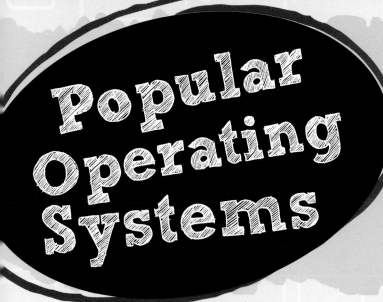

Wow, it's Windows!

Made by Microsoft, Windows are a family of operating systems that includes Windows XP and Windows 7. They are used on about nine out of ten of the world's PCs. Like similar operating systems, they allow you to run more than one application, such as a music player and a word processor, at the same time. This is called **multitasking**.

iOS and MacOS

MacOS was one of the first operating systems to let you use a mouse to click on little pictures called **icons** to open applications. It was designed by Apple to run on its Mac range of computers. Apple's iOS is an operating system for Apple's iPad tablets and iPhones.

Android

Owned by the search engine company Google, Android is the operating system used on over a thousand million smartphones and tablets, as well as some laptops. It lets you **install** little programs called apps (see pages 28–29) quickly and easily.

Bill Gates

Bill Gates showed so much computing promise as a teenager that his school let him skip maths lessons to learn programming. Gates and his school friend, Paul Allen, formed Microsoft in 1975 and released the first Windows operating system ten years later.

It wasn't a big hit, but later versions such as Windows 95, Windows XP and Windows 7 were. Gates was the world's richest man in 2014 with a fortune of over £50 billion!

Keep programming

The teams of programmers that build operating systems don't stop to admire their work once it's released. Instead, they continue working on the operating system, making improvements and fixing things that don't work quite as well as they would like.

A smaller improvement to an operating system is called an **update**. These are often loaded automatically onto a computer, phone or tablet when it connects to the **Internet**. A series of bigger changes to an operating system means a whole new version is released.

TRUE STORY

Sweet Like Sugar Someone working on the Android operating system must have a sweet tooth because all the versions of Android are named after desserts or sweets.

Version 1.5: *Cupcake*
Version 2: *Éclair*
Version 3: *Honeycomb*
Version 4: *Ice Cream Sandwich*
Version 4.1: *Jelly Bean*

Interface to Face

The part of a computer and operating system that you see and interact with – by typing or clicking on commands and files – is called the interface. The first interfaces were made up of text only.

A typical interface

In the past, people had to type in a series of command words and numbers in order to get a computer to do anything. Today, user **interfaces** on computers, tablets and smartphones are much more user-friendly. They vary in style, but most have menus, windows and a cursor, as this example shows.

| Finder | File | Edit | View | Go | Window | Help | | Fri 15.15 |

New Folder
New Folder Window
Open
Open With

Get Info

Duplicate
Make Alias

Move To Trash

The **menu bar** contains lots of program commands. It may appear at the top or side of the screen.

You can move the arrow cursor around the screen to select an object or pick a command.

Clock

Hard Drive

A **drop-down menu** gives you a choice of options within a program. There are different options under each heading.

When you open two or more different files or directories, each one is displayed in its own window on the screen.

English   History   Science

Homework

Pop Music   Soul Music   Reggae Music

Ska Music   R&B Music   Garage Music

Music

Little pictures

The little pictures that you can see on a smartphone, tablet or PC are called icons. These are often used to represent programs. Tapping or clicking on an icon runs the program.

Controlling your computer

On PCs, you move the **cursor** around the screen using a computer mouse, a trackpad or the cursor (arrow) keys on a keyboard. On devices that are fitted with a touchscreen, you touch different parts of the screen to select options.

Drag and drop

On many interfaces, you can click on an item and drag it across the screen. This is known as 'drag and drop'. You may need to do this for lots of reasons, including moving a file or dragging the corner of a window to change its size.

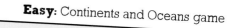

STRETCH YOURSELF

Can You Drag and Drop?

Practise your dragging and dropping skills using a computer mouse, trackpad or touchscreen. Ask an adult to help you type the web links below into a web browser so you can have fun playing these games on the Internet.

Easy: Continents and Oceans game

http://tinyurl.com/drag-globe

Medium: English Language game

http://tinyurl.com/too-big-game

Hard: Properties of Materials Adventure game

http://tinyurl.com/materials-fun

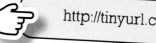

File in Style

Computer data is stored in files. A file can be a piece of music, a recorded TV show, a photograph or perhaps something you have written for school.

Saving files

To work on a document or play a music file, you have to open it. If you make any changes, you need to save the file before closing it. Only close the file after you have saved it, or you will lose your changes.

What's in a name?

When you get a new computer or tablet, it may seem like a good idea to call your first file 'music' or 'letter'. But imagine months later searching through hundreds of files with music or letter in the title – it would take ages to find the right file! That's why it's sensible to use brief words to describe every file you create, such as 'Christmas 2015' for a Christmas wish-list or 'Eiffelsketch' for an Eiffel Tower picture.

File Types

Each file has certain properties, depending on the program or application used to create it. File extensions are a way of labelling a file so your computer can understand what the file contains. The extension .txt, for example, means the file is a simple document that only contains text.

Most file names come in the form: **file name.file extension**. Here are some examples:

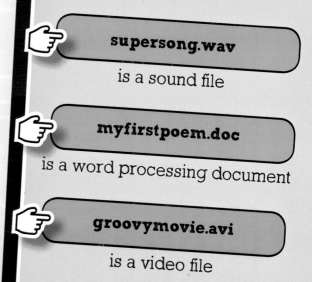

👉 **supersong.wav**

is a sound file

👉 **myfirstpoem.doc**

is a word processing document

👉 **groovymovie.avi**

is a video file

STRETCH YOURSELF

Make the Match

Can you match these examples of different files to their file type?

JPEG
1.

MP3
2.

DOC
3.

MPG
4.

XLS
5.

Answers on page 31

Movie

Letter

Photograph

Data spreadsheet

Music track

File size

Files vary greatly in size. They are measured in bytes, kilobytes, megabytes and gigabytes. A small word processing file may only be 20 kilobytes (KB), while a video file containing a movie may be 600–800 gigabytes (GB) – that's a staggering 30–40,000 times bigger!

Squash me

To make files smaller, you can use file compression applications such as WinZip or Stuffit. A compressed file takes up less memory space and can also take less time to be sent via a computer network such as the Internet.

WARNING!

* Never open a file with an .exe extension because .exe stands for executable. This means that the file is a program that will start running immediately.

* Do not delete a file or move it somewhere else unless you have permission from the owner of the computer.

* Remember to share your personal files only with people you know and trust.

13

Getting Organised

The number of files on a computer can grow quickly as you add new programs, applications and data. But it can be hard to find files if they aren't sorted in some way. That's why you have to get organised!

 A home for files

Files can be organised in folders or **directories**. These are like paper folders in a filing cabinet, with each folder containing different pieces of paper. Your computer files are like these pieces of paper. To sort your files, create new computer folders and give each one a name. For example, you might want to keep photographs and documents in different computer folders.

Folders Inside Folders

Folders are great for organising lots of files. You can put folders of files inside other folders. The folders inside are called sub-folders. For example, if you have schoolwork files in one folder, then you can arrange these files by having a sub-folder for each subject. Inside these sub-folders, you can then have more folders, perhaps sorting your files into school terms.

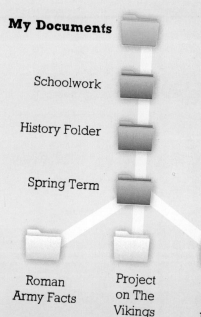

My Documents

Schoolwork

History Folder

Spring Term

Roman Army Facts

Project on The Vikings

Chariot Racing Drawings

Find a file

Once you've organised your files, it is easier to work out what goes where. Most operating systems offer further help. Programs known as file managers let you type in search words. They then list all the files with those search words in their name. File managers let you move files between different folders or make a copy of a file and place it somewhere else. You can also use file managers to sort files in a folder by date, in alphabetical order or by file type.

Back it up

Once your files are organised, you can back them up easily. Backing up means that all your files are copied onto a separate storage device. This may be a **USB pen drive** or an external **hard disk**. Backing up regularly means you will not lose important letters, essays, photographs, music or videos if something goes wrong with your computer.

USB pen drive

STRETCH YOURSELF

Make Your Own Directory Tree

Use a piece of paper to map out your directory tree of folders for storing personal files. Ask yourself the following questions when mapping out the tree:

👉 What folders do you think you will need now and in the future?

👉 How would you split large folders into different sub-folders?

👉 What names could you give each folder so you can remember them later on?

Now ask an adult to help you produce your directory tree on a real computer!

Here is an example to help you:

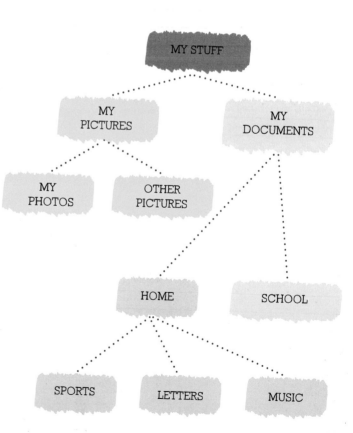

It's the Business

Millions of computers are kept busy every day, working for businesses. They help people to keep track of money, write work reports, count the sales made in a shop, and all sorts of other useful tasks.

Office suites

Computers can run applications such as word processors (see pages 18–19), **spreadsheets**, **databases** and presentation programs. Many home computers have versions of these applications, which are stored in an **office suite**. Microsoft Office is the world's most popular office suite. It has over 1.1 billion users – that's one in seven people on the planet!

Cell by cell

Spreadsheets let you keep, compare and calculate data, which is stored in rows and columns of cells. Changing the information in one cell will update other cells instantly. This makes spreadsheets great for keeping track of money, accounts and sales. Scientists and engineers also use spreadsheets to make difficult calculations.

Information warehouse

Databases let people store information on computers. This information may, for example, be the details of a company's customers or perhaps all the spare parts in a factory. The information is organised so that individual records can be searched for and viewed quickly. You can also easily add new information to a database.

Nice as pie

You can transfer the information stored in databases and spreadsheets to presentation programs. Popular ones include Powerpoint, Prezi and Keynote. Presentation programs help people organise numbers into diagrams, pie charts and graphs, so they can be shown at meetings, talks and school presentations, for example.

Out of the Office

Databases aren't just used in offices. For example, details of criminals and motor vehicles are stored on police databases so that detectives can try to match crime patterns. Libraries also use databases to keep track of books. Your school may also have a database that records how many times you've done well!

Databases help librarians organise and find books.

17

Text Success!

Many people use one application more than any other – a word processor. This lets you write letters, reports and stories by typing into a file called a document.

Work those words!

Microsoft Word, Apache OpenOffice and Apple Pages are popular word processing applications. They are versatile and allow you to create all sorts of different documents, from newspaper pages to birthday cards or menus.

Most word processors have a top menu bar with a File button on the left-hand side. Clicking on this button usually makes a drop-down menu appear, which gives you options. These include opening previous documents, creating a new blank document, or saving a document you're already working on.

SPELLCHECKER IS WRONG!

Most word processors have spelling checkers, but they're often not as good as a dictionary. This is because the computer may not know unusual words or perhaps you've used the wrong word in your text. Oops!

Danny *through* the ball.
(The word should be threw)

Kylie *sore* the bird.
(The word should be saw)

Cut and paste

Before word processors, books and essays were written by hand or typed on a typewriter. They had to be written or typed in the right order and looked messy if mistakes were made. Word processors let you type quickly and make corrections easily. You can also move parts of the writing around by cutting or copying a piece of text and pasting it into a different part of the document.

Font Facts

A font is the style of letters, numbers and other characters in a document. You can pick different fonts in a word processor and also change the **point** size at which they appear in the document. Here are some examples:

☞ This font is called Garamond and the point size is 30 point.

☞ This font is called Helvetica and the point size is 20 point.

Get Typing!
Ask an adult to help you use a word processor application to type a story or poem. Remember you can use the backspace key to correct any mistakes!

Now try the following activities and experiment with presenting your text:

☞ Can you make the title of the story or poem bigger by increasing the size of the font?

☞ Can you find the centre alignment button? Highlight the heading and press the centre button to move the heading to the middle of the page.

☞ Are there any words in your writing that you would like to stand out more – perhaps by putting them in bold or italics?

Text Tools

Whatever font you are using, you can change how it looks by clicking on text tool icons in a word document. These are usually found at the top of the screen.

Bold

Italic

Underline

~~Strikethrough~~

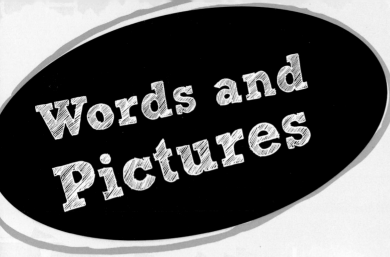

Words and Pictures

Today, most word processing applications are very powerful, letting you do more than just type in words and numbers. They also let you design the page and add images.

Tall or wide?

When you create a new document, you can set up the page to be a certain size and either tall (portrait) or wide (landscape). A4 (29.7cm by 21cm) is the most common page size because most printers handle A4 paper.

Landscape

Portrait

COMPUTER Hero!

Charles Simonyi joined Microsoft in 1981. He worked on a project with Richard Brodie called Multi-Tool Word, which went on sale as Word in 1983. It was the first word processor that could display bold and italic text. It also let users work on more than one document at the same time.

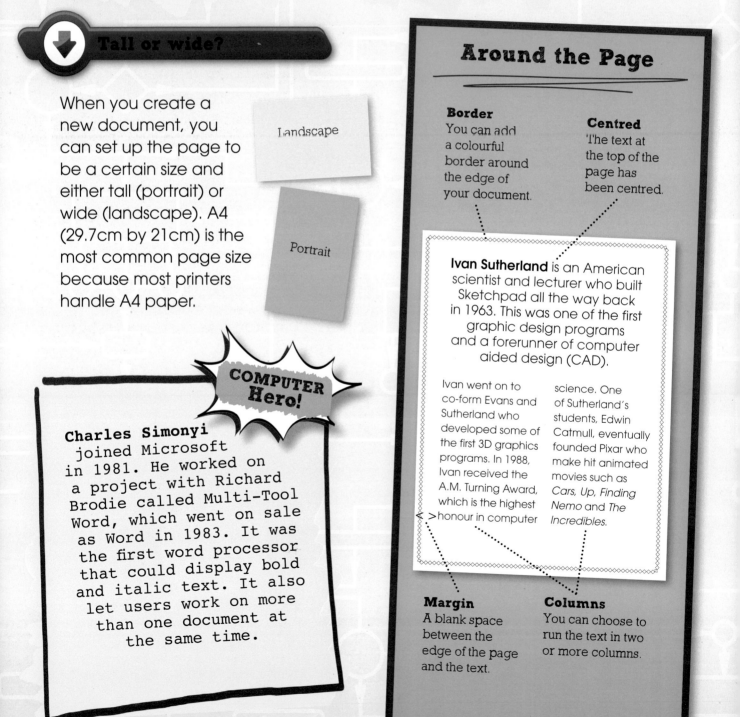

Around the Page

Border
You can add a colourful border around the edge of your document.

Centred
The text at the top of the page has been centred.

Ivan Sutherland is an American scientist and lecturer who built Sketchpad all the way back in 1963. This was one of the first graphic design programs and a forerunner of computer aided design (CAD).

Ivan went on to co-form Evans and Sutherland who developed some of the first 3D graphics programs. In 1988, Ivan received the A.M. Turing Award, which is the highest honour in computer science. One of Sutherland's students, Edwin Catmull, eventually founded Pixar who make hit animated movies such as *Cars, Up, Finding Nemo* and *The Incredibles*.

Margin
A blank space between the edge of the page and the text.

Columns
You can choose to run the text in two or more columns.

Great templates

Most word processors provide templates. These are documents that have already been designed, so you only have to fill in the blanks with your own text. Templates can have borders, pictures and headings already in place. Some are designed as certificates, party invitations or greetings cards.

Adding images

You can add images to word processing documents. This is called **importing** or inserting. The image might be a piece of clip art (a pre-made drawing that comes with the word processor), your own picture or a photograph stored on your computer.

STRETCH YOURSELF

Make a Special Poster
Design a poster to celebrate someone's birthday or another special event. You may find it easier to plan your poster on a piece of paper first.

☞ If you have access to a word processor, work out which commands you'll need to create each part of the poster – perhaps a change of font colour, centring or a word wrap?

☞ Do you know how to import a picture or a piece of clip art into the poster?

☞ Ask an adult to help you print the poster. It will look amazing, especially if you use a colour printer.

It's a wrap!

To get your document looking good, you may have to change the size of the imported image. You may also have to decide where the text should go in the document. Most word processors let you wrap text so that the text surrounds an image. Without any wrapping, the text would run over the picture and cover it up.

Sounds and Music

The world of computing would be very quiet without sound applications! Some of these react to voice commands, while others let musicians play, record and edit their music.

Record, play, enjoy!

Most operating systems feature sound recorder and sound player applications. A microphone, built into a smartphone or connected to a computer, converts the sound into electrical signals. These are then turned into computer data and stored as a **sound file.**

Other applications let you edit sound files. For example, you may wish to change the pitch of the notes, cut certain bits out or add special sound effects. You can then save and play back the sound file.

Shrinking sounds

There are lots of types of sound file, with funny names such as FLAC, WAV and Ogg Vorbis! One of the most popular is called an MP3. This is a form of file compression (see page 13). When a program converts sound into an MP3 file, it removes some of the data, such as sounds that are too low or high for us to hear, in order to make the file much smaller.

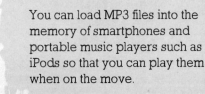

You can load MP3 files into the memory of smartphones and portable music players such as iPods so that you can play them when on the move.

TRUE STORY

Jackpot! When Alex Ostrovsky downloaded a song by the band Coldplay, he couldn't have guessed what would happen next. Alex's download was the billionth on iTunes and so Apple sent him a brand new computer, 10 iPod music players and a $10,000 gift card... Result!

On track

People used to buy vinyl albums to listen to music. Today, millions of people get their music from the Internet by **downloading** MP3 and other sound files. Music stores like Apple's iTunes offer tracks for sale in this way, with an average of 15,000 songs being downloaded every minute of every day in 2013.

 Making music

Some music applications can turn tablets and smartphones into guitars, pianos or other instruments. Other applications turn laptops and PCs into recording studios, so that musicians can mix the different parts of their music at home.

STRETCH YOURSELF

Make Some Sounds!
Have a short history lesson about the first computer music and then treat yourself to an exciting drumming experience.

👉 Type the following link into a web browser to hear the oldest surviving recording of a computer playing tunes – a 1951 Ferranti Mark 1 computer playing 'God Save The Queen' and 'Ba Ba Black Sheep'!

> http://tinyurl.com/oldest-tune

👉 Type the following link into a web browser to turn your computer keyboard into a cool virtual drum kit.

> http://tinyurl.com/drums-on-screen

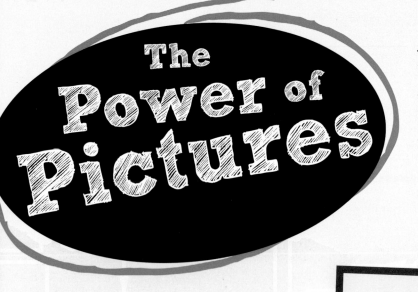

The Power of Pictures

As computers have increased in power, some clever applications have been developed that let you use a computer to produce designs, works of art and animated movies.

Photo fun

Smartphones and digital cameras contain programs that process images taken with their camera lens. Some let you apply special effects, such as removing the red-eye caused by flash photography or turning a colour photograph into a black-and-white one.

Image Editors

Image editors are applications such as Photoshop or Photoplus that allow changes to photos or images. For example, you can make photographs lighter or darker, or increase the difference between the darkest and lightest parts. This is called contrast.

Original photograph

The small tree has been removed.

The brightness of the sky has been increased.

The outer edges of the photograph have been removed to get a close-up view. This is called cropping.

Artists use illustration applications to produce all sorts of artwork. These allow them to change their artwork easily. Many objects, such as cars and clothing, are designed on computers using powerful **CAD** (Computer Aided Design) programs. These enable designers, architects and engineers to produce highly accurate drawings and plans of their products.

Special effects

Some image editing applications let you apply amazing and convincing effects such as making funny faces. You can even merge photographs, perhaps putting a person from one photograph into a completely different scene.

Movie magic

Video editing applications let movie-makers edit the footage taken with their cameras, add a soundtrack and even apply special effects such as slow motion. Professional movie-makers use powerful programs to create computer-generated images of all sorts of things, from aliens to giant armies.

TRUE STORY

Shark Attack! Don't believe everything that you see. A photograph of a giant shark attacking a helicopter became popular on websites in the early 2000s. It turned out to be a trick — created by putting together separate photographs of a shark taken in South Africa with a helicopter photo from the USA.

Games, Games, Games

People played the first computer games on big machines in games arcades. As computing advanced, games became popular at home on machines called games consoles, and later on PCs, tablets and smartphones.

Playing games

Computer games are now sold in huge numbers. For example, by October 2014, over 54 million copies of Minecraft had been sold, while the Mario and Super Mario series of action games have sold a staggering 445 million copies!

Games come in a dizzying number of different types, which are known as genres. Some are strategy or puzzle games. These challenge your brain as you try to find a solution. Others are action-adventure games where players control a character travelling through a world, solving problems and avoiding dangers.

TRUE STORY

Many Minds Today, computer games are created by huge teams of designers and programmers. They can be very expensive, too. For example, did you know that Disney's Infinity computer game cost as much as $100 million to produce?

Computer fairs give gamers an opportunity to try out the latest software and technology.

TRUE STORY

Start Young! Christopher Purdy wrote a computer game called Smiley Dodgems when he was only 13 years old. The game won a BAFTA Games Designer award in 2012 and Christopher got the chance to work with professional computer game designers. Cool!

Serious fun

Some games are just for fun, but others have a serious purpose. Games can be used to teach children and adults a foreign language or to improve their typing skills. Quizzes can improve people's knowledge of history or geography, whilst some games teach important science topics by letting users perform experiments on screen.

Simulate and educate

Simulation games mirror real-life situations or skills, such as keeping a pet or driving a car. Some simulations are used for real-life training. For example, pilots can learn to fly using powerful flight simulator programs.

COMPUTER Heroes!

Dona Bailey helped write a popular Atari arcade game called Centipede and Roberta Williams created the first-ever graphical adventure game Mystery House and the King's Quest series of adventures.

Early Atari computer game

App Attack!

Apps are small applications that are designed to work on mobile computer devices such as tablets and smartphones. They usually perform only one task.

Get the app you want?

Most apps are downloaded wirelessly using a smartphone or tablet to connect to a computer network. Other apps called **web apps** are based online and can only be accessed by a device with Internet access.

What's in store?

Apps can be found in stores such as Apple's App store or Google's Play store for devices that use the Android operating system. In 2009, there were 2,300 different apps in the Android Market. As of August 2014, the Google Play store contained 1.3 million apps!

Top of the apps

Many websites have their own apps, which makes using their services easier. These apps are designed for the small screens of smartphones. Games are among the most popular apps of all. Apps rise and fall in popularity, but one of the most popular is Angry Birds. By early 2014, it had been downloaded two billion times from the Google Play store.

Red Bird has featured in every version of the popular Angry Birds game.

Free and easy

Almost a million apps on Google Play are free, but many let you use only some of the app's features. This is so you will buy the full version if you like it enough. Remember: never download an app without permission. Always ask first!

STRETCH YOURSELF

Doodle and Draw
If you enjoy drawing pictures and looking at amazing paintings, then have some fun exploring these arty websites:

Type doodle.ly into a web browser to visit a fun drawing web app. Click the Doodle Now button (top right) and draw your own doodle.

Head to the National Gallery of Art's collection of web apps by typing the address below into your web browser. There, you can make portraits, turn images into cartoons and much more.

http://tinyurl.com/kids-art-apps

Glossary

application A computer program or group of programs that help a user perform a specific task.

booting up The starting up process of a computer system, often performed by a computer's operating system.

CAD (Computer Aided Design) The use of computers to design plans and help engineers produce technical drawings of machines or buildings.

code A set of clear, step-by-step instructions for programming a computer so that it can perform specific tasks.

cursor A moving symbol, such as an arrow, which indicates a position on a computer's screen.

database A program that allows people to store huge amounts of information on computers with ease.

directory A folder that holds a collection of files on a computer.

download To request and receive a file, sometimes a program or app, from another computer.

drop-down menu Used in many programs, this gives the list of options available in a menu bar.

hard disk A memory storage device made up of many magnetic discs that can store lots of data.

icon A small picture displayed on screen that opens the file or runs the program when selected.

importing To add a file, such as a photograph or diagram, to another document.

install Load and get a program ready to run on a computer.

interface A program or part of an operating system that lets you communicate with a computer. The interface displays information on screen and lets you type or click to give commands to the computer.

Internet A network that connects millions of computers all over the world.

menu bar A row of options that usually appears along the top or side of the screen.

microprocessor A silicon chip that performs all a computer's calculations and also controls its other parts.

multitasking Performing more than one task on a computer at the same time.

office suite A collection of programs that lets you perform different tasks, such as word processing, making spreadsheets and creating presentations.

operating system The programs that run a computer's basic functions and manage other programs running on the system.

point The measurement of the size of a font. A point is just 0.35mm high. Lots of documents use 10, 12 or 14 point fonts. Titles or headings use larger point sizes.

program A set of instructions that can be carried out on a computer or digital device.

sound file A computer file containing music, speech or other sounds that can be played on a device such as a tablet or iPod.

spreadsheet An application that creates documents full of information in rows and columns, which can be easily altered and used in maths, science or business.

update A file that contains new information and small changes (known as fixes) to an application, which are downloaded and run to ensure an application works well.

USB pen drive A portable memory storage device that connects to a computer or tablet using a USB port.

web app A small program that runs on a web page or in a web browser.

Further Resources

Books

Future Science Now: What's Next For Communication?
by Tom Jackson (Wayland, 2013)

Quick Expert's Guide: Computing and Programming
by Shahneila Saeed (Wayland, 2015)

High-Tech Science: How Does a Touch Screen Work?
by Leon Gray (Wayland, 2015)

Big Business: Microsoft
by Cath Senker (Wayland, 2013)

Websites

http://www.sciencemuseum.org.uk/online_science/explore_our_collections/information_age
Learn how computers have become part of everyday life.

http://www.brainpop.co.uk/designandtechnology/computing
Explore the amazing world of computer technology.

http://www.bbc.co.uk/guides/z9r72hv
Discover different ways to communicate using the Internet.

www.bbc.co.uk/guides/z8yk87h
Fun interactive website about databases.

http://www.bbc.co.uk/guides/zxgq7ty
A step-by-step guide to building your own app.

http://www.carnegiecyberacademy.com/
Fun games and lots of tips for keeping safe when using computers.

Answers

page 13 Make the Match:
1. The .jpg file is the photograph.
2. The .mp3 file is the music track.
3. The .doc file is the letter.
4. The .mpg file is the movie.
5. The .xls file is the data spreadsheet.

Index